52 DECLARATIONS

FOR A LIFE ROOTED IN TRUTH

52 SCRIPTURES AND DECLARATIONS
OF FAITH, HEALING, AND WHOLENESS

COLLEEN IAMMARINO

52 Declarations
For a Life Rooted in Truth

52 Scriptures and Declarations of
Faith, Healing, and Wholeness

By Colleen Iammarino

This devotional belongs to

____

Date Started ____________

Copyright Page
52 Declarations Devotional
by Colleen Iammarino

Published by Davcol Publishing
P.O. Box 7132
Woodland Park, CO 80863-0200
United States

www.MondayMorningMinistry.co
Email: info@mondaymorningministry.co

Printed in the United States of America
First Printing: June 2025

Editing by MessageLaunchProgram.com
Book cover by Tannera Lindvall

Interior design by Tannera Lindvall

Table of Contents

Growing in Faith

&

Trusting God's Faithfulness

As you begin this first section, you'll discover Scriptures and declarations that remind you of God's unwavering faithfulness. Each passage is chosen to strengthen your faith, anchor your heart in His promises, and encourage you to trust Him more deeply in every season of life. As you read and declare these truths, let them build confidence that God is who He says He is—and that His Word will never fail.

Declaration

One

Scripture
"He was fully assured that what God promised, He was able to perform." – Romans 4:21

Declaration
I walk by faith and not by sight. I take God at His Word. His promises are true in my life!

Declaration

Two

Scripture
"Now faith is the substance of things hoped for,
the evidence of things not seen."
– Hebrews 11:1

Declaration
My faith is growing! I trust in what God has
already done, and I receive His promises today!

<h1 style="text-align:center">Declaration</h1>
<h1 style="text-align:center">Three</h1>

Scripture
"And He went up into the boat with them, and the wind ceased (sank to rest as if exhausted by its own beating). And they were astonished exceedingly [beyond measure]..." – Mark 6:51 (AMP Classic Edition)

Declaration
I am never alone. Jesus is in my boat, and the winds must cease!

Declaration

Four

Scripture

"Come to Me, all you who labor and are heavy laden, and I will give you rest. Take My yoke upon you and learn from Me, for I am gentle and lowly in heart, and you will find rest for your souls. For My yoke is easy and My burden is light." – Matthew 11:28-30 (NKJV)

Declaration

I am walking in His rest. His yoke is easy, His burden is light, and I am fully pleasing to Him!

Declaration

Five

Scripture
"That He would grant you, according to the riches of His glory, to be strengthened with might through His Spirit in the inner man." – Ephesians 3:16

Declaration
I am strong in the Lord and in the power of His might! The Mighty One lives in me!

Declaration

Six

Scripture

"Trust in the Lord with all your heart; do not depend on your own understanding. Seek his will in all you do, and he will show you which path to take. Don't be impressed with your own wisdom. Instead, fear the Lord and turn away from evil. Then you will have healing for your body and strength for your bones." – Proverbs 3:5-8

Declaration

I trust in the Lord with all my heart. I do not lean on my own understanding. His wisdom leads me into joy, peace, and strength!

Declaration Seven

Scripture
"But You, O Lord, are a shield for me, my glory, and the lifter of my head. With my voice I cry to the Lord, and He hears and answers me out of His holy hill. Selah [pause, and calmly think of that]!" – Psalm 3:3-4 (AMPC)

Declaration
God is my shield! He surrounds me, protects me, and lifts my head in victory!

Declaration

Eight

Scripture

"For in the time of trouble He shall hide me in His pavilion; in the secret place of His tabernacle He shall hide me; He shall set me high upon a rock." – Psalm 27:5 (NKJV)

Declaration

I dwell in the secret place of the Most High. I am covered, protected, and hidden in Him!

Declaration

Nine

Scripture

"Now hope does not disappoint, because the love of God has been poured out in our hearts by the Holy Spirit who was given to us." – Romans 5:5 (NKJV)

Declaration

I am rooted and grounded in God's love. His love has been poured into my heart, and it never fails!

Declaration

Ten

Scripture

"So consider carefully how Jesus faced such intense opposition from sinners who opposed their own souls, so that you won't become worn down and cave in under life's pressures." – Hebrews 12:3 (TPT)

Declaration

I do not quit! I am strong in the Lord, filled with His power, and I walk in victory!

Declaration

Eleven

Scripture
"Ask, and it will be given to you; seek, and you will find; knock, and it will be opened to you. For everyone who asks receives, and he who seeks finds, and to him who knocks it will be opened." – Matthew 7:7-8 (NKJV)

Declaration
God hears me when I call! I have confidence that He answers me, and I walk in His wisdom every day.

Declaration

Twelve

Scripture
"So shall My word be that goes forth from My mouth; It shall not return to Me void, But it shall accomplish what I please, And it shall prosper in the thing for which I sent it."
– Isaiah 55:11 (NKJV)

Declaration
There is NOTHING too hard for my God! His Word is settled, His promises are sure, and I walk in His faithfulness!

Declaration

Thirteen

Scripture
"But of Him you are in Christ Jesus, who became for us wisdom from God—and righteousness and sanctification and redemption." – 1 Corinthians 1:30 (NKJV)

Declaration
Jesus is my wisdom, my righteousness, my sanctification, and my redemption. In Him, I lack nothing!

Declaration

Fourteen

Scripture
"Keep your heart with all diligence, for out of it
spring the issues of life." – Proverbs 4:23 (NKJV)

Declaration
I guard my heart with God's Word! I refuse to
let fear take root, and I choose to walk in His joy
and peace!

Walking in Freedom, Truth, and Victory

This next section is designed to remind you of the freedom Christ has already secured for you. The Scriptures and declarations here will help you stand firm in His truth and walk daily in the victory He has promised. As you meditate on God's Word and speak these declarations over your life, let them break off fear, doubt, and lies—replacing them with confidence, clarity, and strength in Him.

Declaration

Fifteen

Scripture
"He will rescue you from every hidden trap of the enemy, and He will protect you from false accusation and any deadly curse. His massive arms are wrapped around you, protecting you. You can run under His covering of majesty and hide. His arms of faithfulness are a shield keeping you from harm." – Psalm 91:3-4 (TPT)

Declaration
I am free from every trap of the enemy! Fear has no hold on me—I trust in the Lord, and He keeps me safe!

Declaration

Sixteen

Scripture
"The law of the Lord is perfect, converting the soul." – Psalm 19:7a (NKJV)

Declaration
God's Word transforms and restores me! I am not stuck—I am being renewed daily in His truth!

Declaration

Seventeen

Scripture
"The testimony of the Lord is sure, making wise the simple." – Psalm 19:7b (NKJV)

Declaration
God's Word is my wisdom! I treasure His truth above all else, and my life is being transformed daily!

Declaration

Eighteen

Scripture
"O clap your hands, all you people; Shout to God with the voice of triumph and songs of joy." – Psalm 47:1 (AMP)

Declaration
I shout with the voice of triumph! Victory is mine, joy is mine, and my praise silences the enemy!

Declaration

Nineteen

Scripture
"They are not of the world, just as I am not of the world." – John 17:16 (NKJV)

Declaration
I live by faith, not by sight! I am a new creation, seated in heavenly places, and I walk in the reality of God's Kingdom!

Declaration

Twenty

Scripture
"But these are the ones sown on good ground, those who hear the word, accept it, and bear fruit: some thirtyfold, some sixty, and some a hundred." – Mark 4:20 (NKJV)

Declaration
I plant the incorruptible seed of God's Word in my heart, and I will reap a harvest of blessing!

Declaration

Twenty - One

Scripture
"Wisdom is the principal thing; therefore get wisdom. And in all your getting, get understanding." – Proverbs 4:7 (NKJV)

Declaration
I have the wisdom of God! I walk in revelation, understanding, and divine direction every day!

Declaration

Twenty - Two

Scripture
"He refreshes and restores my soul (life); He leads me in the paths of righteousness for His name's sake." – Psalm 23:3 (AMP)

Declaration
I am refreshed by the presence of the Lord! His Word renews my heart, strengthens my soul, and restores my joy!

Declaration

Twenty - Three

Scripture
"And you, being dead in your trespasses, He has made alive (quickened) together with Him, having forgiven you all trespasses." – Colossians 2:13 (NKJV)

Declaration
I am quickened by the Spirit of God! His resurrection power flows through me, giving me life, strength, and renewal every day!

Declaration

Twenty - Four

Scripture
"For with God nothing [is or ever] shall be impossible." Then Mary said, "Behold, I am the servant of the Lord; may it be done to me according to your word." And the angel left her." – Luke 1:37-38 (AMP)

Declaration
With God, nothing is impossible! I believe His Word, and I receive His promises in my life!

Declaration

Twenty - Five

Scripture
"And you, being dead in your trespasses and the uncircumcision of your flesh, He has made alive together with Him, having forgiven you all trespasses." – Colossians 2:13 (NKJV)

Declaration
I am completely forgiven! My sins are wiped away, and I walk in freedom and righteousness every day!

Declaration

Twenty - Six

Scripture

"For He made Him who knew no sin to be sin for us, that we might become the righteousness of God in Him." – 2 Corinthians 5:21 (NKJV)

Declaration

I am the righteousness of God in Christ! I have bold access to my Father, and I live in peace, quietness, and assurance forever!

Living in the Healing Reality of God's Kingdom

God's Kingdom is marked by wholeness, restoration, and life. In this section, the Scriptures and declarations focus on the healing that flows from His presence and the promises He has made to His children. As you take in these truths and declare them over your body, mind, and spirit, allow faith to rise in you for the reality of His Kingdom to manifest in your life. His Word is alive, and His healing power is for you today.

Declaration

Twenty - Seven

Scripture
"I led them gently with cords of a man, with bonds of love [guiding them], and I was to them as one who lifts up and eases the yoke [of the law] over their jaws; and I bent down to them and fed them." – Hosea 11:4 (AMP)

Declaration
God has already healed and delivered me! I refuse to carry burdens that have been removed—I walk in freedom every day!

Declaration

Twenty – Eight

Scripture
"Surely, He has borne our griefs (sicknesses, weaknesses, and distresses) and carried our sorrows and pains [of punishment]. Yet we ignorantly considered Him stricken, smitten, and afflicted by God. But He was wounded for our transgressions, He was bruised for our guilt and iniquities; the chastisement [needful to obtain] peace and well-being for us was upon Him, and with the stripes [that wounded] Him we are healed and made whole." – Isaiah 53:4-5 (AMP)

Declaration
Healing is God's will for me! I reject sickness and receive the fullness of His healing power in my life!

<h1 style="text-align:center">Declaration</h1>

<h1 style="text-align:center">Twenty - Nine</h1>

Scripture

"My help comes from the Lord, who made heaven and earth. He will not allow your foot to slip; He who keeps you will not slumber. Behold, He who keeps Israel will neither slumber nor sleep. The Lord is your keeper; The Lord is your shade on your right hand. The sun will not strike you by day, nor the moon by night. The Lord will protect you from all evil; He will keep your life. The Lord will guard your going out and your coming in [everything that you do] from this time forth and forever." – Psalm 121:2-8 (AMP)

Declaration

I am protected by the Lord! I will not fear, for He is my shield, my fortress, and my helper. With a

long life, He will satisfy me!

Declaration

Thirty

Scripture

"Bless the Lord, O my soul, and forget not all His benefits: Who forgives all your iniquities, Who heals all your diseases, Who redeems your life from destruction, Who crowns you with loving-kindness and tender mercies, Who satisfies your mouth with good things, So that your youth is renewed like the eagle's." – Psalm 103:2-5 (NKJV)

Declaration

I receive ALL the benefits of God! I am forgiven, healed, redeemed, crowned, satisfied, and renewed in Christ!

Declaration

Thirty - One

Scripture

"O Lord God of our fathers, are You not God in heaven, and do You not rule over all the kingdoms of the nations, and in Your hand is there not power and might, so that no one is able to withstand You?" – 2 Chronicles 20:6 (NKJV)

Declaration

I am righteous. I am strong. I am immovable. I withstand the enemy and stand in victory with truth, peace, faith, and salvation. I give my full attention to God's Word, and I triumph in every confrontation.

Declaration

Thirty - Two

Scripture

"These things I have spoken to you, that in Me you may have peace. In the world you will have tribulation; but be of good cheer, I have overcome the world." – John 16:33 (NKJV)

Declaration

I am strong, I am courageous, and I am full of faith! I refuse to fear because Jesus has already overcome the world!

Declaration

Thirty – Three

Scripture
"Ask, and it will be given to you; seek, and you will find; knock, and it will be opened to you. For everyone who asks receives, and he who seeks finds, and to him who knocks it will be opened." – Matthew 7:7-8 (NKJV)

Declaration
Healing and wisdom flow from within me! I am connected to the source of life, and I walk in divine health and revelation!

Declaration

Thirty - Four

Scripture
"Christ redeemed us from that self-defeating, cursed life by absorbing it completely into Himself... And now, because of that, the air is cleared, and we can see that Abraham's blessing is present and available for us all."–Galatians 3:13-14 (MSG)

Declaration
I am already healthy! Healing belongs to me, and I walk in divine health every day!

Declaration

Thirty - Five

Scripture
"He did not waver at the promise of God
through unbelief, but was strengthened in faith,
giving glory to God, and being fully convinced
that what He had promised He was also able to
perform."
– Romans 4:20-21 (NKJV)

Declaration
I am fully persuaded in God's promises! I reject
lies, renew my mind, and walk in the truth of
who I am in Christ!

Declaration

Thirty - Six

Scripture
"He will be standing firm like a flourishing tree planted by God's design, deeply rooted by the brooks of bliss, bearing fruit in every season of his life. He is never dry, never fainting, ever blessed, ever prosperous." – Psalm 1:3 (TPT)

Declaration
I am planted, strong, and flourishing! I am rooted in the Word, and everything I do prospers!

Declaration

Thirty-Seven

Scripture
"That you may be filled [through all your being] unto all the fullness of God, that you may have the richest measure of the Divine Presence, and become a body wholly filled and flooded with God Himself!" – Ephesians 3:19 (AMP)

Declaration
The Kingdom of God is in me and surrounds me! I walk in the supply of healing, provision, and wisdom every day!

<h1 style="text-align:center">Declaration</h1>

<h1 style="text-align:center">Thirty - Eight</h1>

Scripture

"The Lord is my shepherd; I have all that I need. He lets me rest in green meadows; He leads me beside peaceful streams. He renews my strength. He guides me along right paths, bringing honor to His name." – Psalm 23:1-3 (NLT)

Declaration

The Lord is my Shepherd—I have everything I need! I walk in healing, peace, and strength every day!

Declaration

Thirty - Nine

Scripture
"Thanks be to God, who gives us the victory through our Lord Jesus Christ. Therefore, my beloved brethren, be steadfast, immovable, always abounding in the work of the Lord, knowing that your labor is not in vain in the Lord." – 1 Corinthians 15:57-58 (NKJV)

Declaration
I stand firm in faith! I will not be moved by what I see, but by what I know—God's promises are already mine!

Living in Your True Identity in Christ

In Christ, you are fully known, fully loved, and completely made new. This last section of Scriptures and declarations will remind you of who you are in Him—not defined by past mistakes or the opinions of others, but by the truth of God's Word. As you read and declare these promises, let them renew your mind and anchor your heart in the unshakable reality of your identity as a child of God, equipped and empowered to live with purpose.

Declaration

Forty

Scripture
"Bless the Lord, O my soul, and forget not all His benefits: Who forgives all your iniquities, Who heals all your diseases, Who redeems your life from destruction, Who crowns you with lovingkindness and tender mercies, Who satisfies your mouth with good things, so that your youth is renewed like the eagle's." – Psalm 103:2-5 (NKJV)

Declaration
I remember all the Lord's benefits! I am forgiven, healed, redeemed, and renewed every day!

Declaration

Forty - One

Scripture
"But God demonstrates His own love toward us, in that while we were still sinners, Christ died for us." – Romans 5:8 (NKJV)

Declaration
I am loved unconditionally by God! His love is not based on my performance—it is based on who He is!

Forty – Two

Scripture
"But we all, with unveiled face, beholding as in a mirror the glory of the Lord, are being transformed into the same image from glory to glory, just as by the Spirit of the Lord."
– 2 Corinthians 3:18 (NKJV)

Declaration
I see myself through the mirror of God's Word! I am who He says I am, and I walk in victory!

Declaration

Forty - Three

Scripture
"For you did not receive the spirit of bondage again to fear, but you received the Spirit of adoption by whom we cry out, 'Abba, Father.'" – Romans 8:15 (NKJV)

Declaration
I have been brought near by the blood of Jesus. I am adopted, redeemed, and made whole. I live as a child of God, fully accepted and fully loved.

Declaration

Forty - Four

Scripture
"For the weapons of our warfare are not carnal but mighty in God for pulling down strongholds, casting down arguments and every high thing that exalts itself against the knowledge of God, bringing every thought into captivity to the obedience of Christ, and being ready to punish all disobedience when your obedience is fulfilled."
– 2 Corinthians 10:4-6 (NKJV)

Declaration
I take every thought captive! I am renewing my mind daily, pulling down strongholds, and walking in the victory of God's truth!

Declaration

Forty - Five

Scripture
"He has delivered us from the power of darkness and conveyed us into the kingdom of the Son of His love." – Colossians 1:13 (NKJV)

Declaration
I am fully loved, fully forgiven, and fully restored in Christ. I walk in the fullness of my Father's love!

Declaration

Forty - Six

Scripture
"There is therefore now no condemnation to those who are in Christ Jesus."
– Romans 8:1 (NKJV)

Declaration
I am fully loved, fully forgiven, and fully restored in Christ. My past is gone, my future is secure, and I walk in the fullness of my Father's love!

Declaration

Forty - Seven

Scripture
"Behold, I am the Lord, the God of all flesh. Is there anything too hard for Me?"
– Jeremiah 32:27 (NKJV)

Declaration
I take the limits off God! I believe in His power, trust in His promises, and expect great things in my life!

Declaration

Forty - Eight

Scripture

"For we are His workmanship [His own master work, a work of art], created in Christ Jesus [reborn from above—spiritually transformed, renewed, ready to be used] for good works, which God prepared [for us] beforehand [taking paths which He set], so that we would walk in them [living the good life which He prearranged and made ready for us]." – Ephesians 2:10 (AMP)

Declaration

I am God's masterpiece! I walk in my purpose, fulfill my calling, and live in the identity God has given me!

Declaration

Forty - Nine

Scripture
"and the peace of God, which surpasses all understanding, will guard your hearts and minds
through Christ Jesus." – Philippians 4:7 (NKJV)

Declaration
I have a sound mind! I reject fear, embrace faith,
and walk in the peace and power of God!

Declaration

Fifty

Scripture
"Love has been perfected among us in this: that we may have boldness in the day of judgment; because as He is, so are we in this world." – 1 John 4:17 (NKJV)

Declaration
The Greater One lives in me! I walk in victory, power, and boldness because Jesus is in me!

Declaration

Fifty - One

Scripture
"May the God of hope fill you with all joy and peace in believing [through the experience of your faith] that by the power of the Holy Spirit you will abound in hope and overflow with confidence in His promises." – Romans 15:13 (AMP)

Declaration
I fix my eyes on God's truth! His Word is my focus, His promises are my foundation, and His peace fills my heart!

Declaration

Fifty - Two

Scripture
"And you are complete in Him, who is the head
of all principality and power."
– Colossians 2:10 (NKJV)

Declaration
I am complete in Christ! I lack nothing, and I
walk in the fullness of my identity in Him!

Remember:

You are *Loved,*

you are *Righteous,*

and you are *His!*

About the Author & Speaker

Invite Colleen Iammarino to Your Church or Event

Colleen Iammarino is a wife, mom, and grandmother whose life overflows with the goodness of God. As a minister, speaker, and author, she shares her journey as a living testimony of His healing power and unconditional love. After battling years of debilitating pain caused by Reflex Sympathetic Dystrophy, Colleen experienced a miraculous healing that transformed her life. Today, she shares that journey to help others walk in healing, wholeness, and their divine identity through the finished work of Christ.

Alongside her husband, David, she leads Monday Morning Ministry, a platform offering weekly devotionals and teachings that anchor believers in truth and strengthen their faith. Her message centers on God's grace, teaching that true healing begins in the heart and flows into every area of life. Colleen is also a featured speaker on *Healing Journeys Today* and and also teaches on Andrew Wommack's Gospel Truth Network, encouraging audiences worldwide with her story of faith and victory.

Why Invite Colleen?

- **Inspiring Testimony**: Her healing story reveals the power of God's Word to restore spirit, soul, and body.
- **Biblical, Heart-Centered Teaching**: She shares truth with clarity, love, and spiritual authority.
- **Experienced & Relatable**: With a background in digital tech and ministry, she connects with a wide range of audiences.
- **Global Encourager**: Her message reaches believers around the world, offering hope and transformation.

Bring Colleen to Your Next Event

If you're seeking a speaker who will stir faith, minister healing, and ignite identity in Christ—Colleen would be honored to serve your church or ministry event.

Booking Information

Visit: www.mondaymorningministry.co
Email: info@mondaymorningministry.co

**Partner with Us
to Spread Healing
and Hope**

We are delighted that our ministry has blessed you! Your partnership enables us to continue sharing messages of healing and hope with those who have yet to hear. Together, we can reach more hearts and transform more lives.

Ways to Support Our Ministry:

- **Online Donations:** Visit our website's Giving Page to make a secure online donation at https://mondaymorningministry.co/giving/

- **Mail-In Contributions:** You can mail your donations to:

Monday Morning Ministry
P.O. Box 7132
Woodland Park, CO 80863-0200

- **Support Through Healing Journeys Today:** Partner with us via the <u>Healing Journeys Today</u> platform.

Your Generosity Makes a Difference

Your support allows us to:

- **Expand Our Outreach:** Bringing the message of God's love and healing power to new audiences.

- **Develop Resources:** Creating materials that inspire faith and encourage spiritual growth.

- **Host Events:** Organizing conferences and workshops that foster community and deepen understanding of God's promises.

We are deeply grateful for your partnership. Together, we can continue spreading the life-changing message of healing and hope to those around the world who have yet to hear it.

Blessings,
Colleen and David Iammarino
Founder, Monday Morning Ministry